Visit www.CristinApril.com and sign up to join the Colorholics Anonymous Club for free! You will receive a monthly coloring page, coupon codes, coloring tips & tricks, the newest updates, and much more!

Share your completed colorings and connect with me!

Facebook: www.facebook.com/CristinAprilsArt
Pinterest: www.pinterest.com/cristinapril
Instagram: @cristinapril
Twitter: @cristinapril

Printable pages are available in my shop at

www.CristinApril.etsy.com

This book is dedicated to my favorite husband who puts up with my incessant working and understanding of all the times I can be looking straight at him and not hear a word he said. Thank you for being supportive, making me laugh, and bearing my sass. I love you, today!

Thank you to Rachel Gillham who colored the cover of this book.

About the Author:
Cristin is a self-taught artist who loves lettering, doodling, and sarcasm.
She has combined these into hand-drawn coloring pages for others to enjoy. Cristin resides in upstate New York with her rescue beagle, rescue husband, her daughter, and a lot of coffee and wine.

The Art of Not Giving A Fuck by Cristin April Frey

Colorist: _____Date: _____

Medium Used: _____

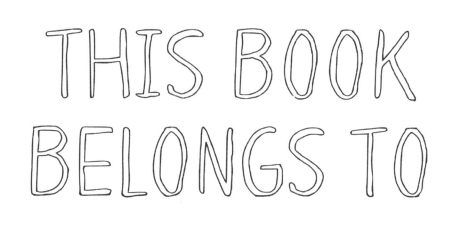

THIS BOOK BELONGS TO

_____

AND I DON'T GIVE A FUCK!

The Art of Not Giving A Fuck by Cristin April Frey

Colorist: _____Date: _____

Medium Used: _____

Today's Recipe:

2 cups cluster

1 cup fuck

crushandpris.com

The Art of Not Giving A Fuck by Cristin April Frey

Colorist: _____ Date: _____

Medium Used: _____

THE PATH TO INNER PEACE BEGINS WITH FOUR WORDS...

NOT MY FUCKING PROBLEM

CristinApril.com

The Art of Not Giving A Fuck by Cristin April Frey

Colorist: _____Date: _____

Medium Used: _____

Giving a fuck doesn't really go with my outfit.

The Art of Not Giving A Fuck by Cristin April Frey

Colorist: _____Date: _____

Medium Used: _____

KristinApril.com

The Art of Not Giving A Fuck by Cristin April Frey

Colorist: _____Date: _____

Medium Used: _____

You know what that sounds like? Not my fucking problem.

CristinApril.com

The Art of Not Giving A Fuck by Cristin April Frey

Colorist: _____Date: _____

Medium Used: _____

The Art of Not Giving A Fuck by Cristin April Frey

Colorist: _____Date: _____

Medium Used: _____

The Art of Not Giving A Fuck by Cristin April Frey

Colorist: _____Date: _____

Medium Used: _____

No, really... It's adorable when you think I give a shit.

The Art of Not Giving A Fuck by Cristin April Frey

Colorist: _____ Date: _____

Medium Used: _____

The Art of Not Giving A Fuck by Cristin April Frey

Colorist: _____Date: _____

Medium Used: _____

My favorite color is fuck you.

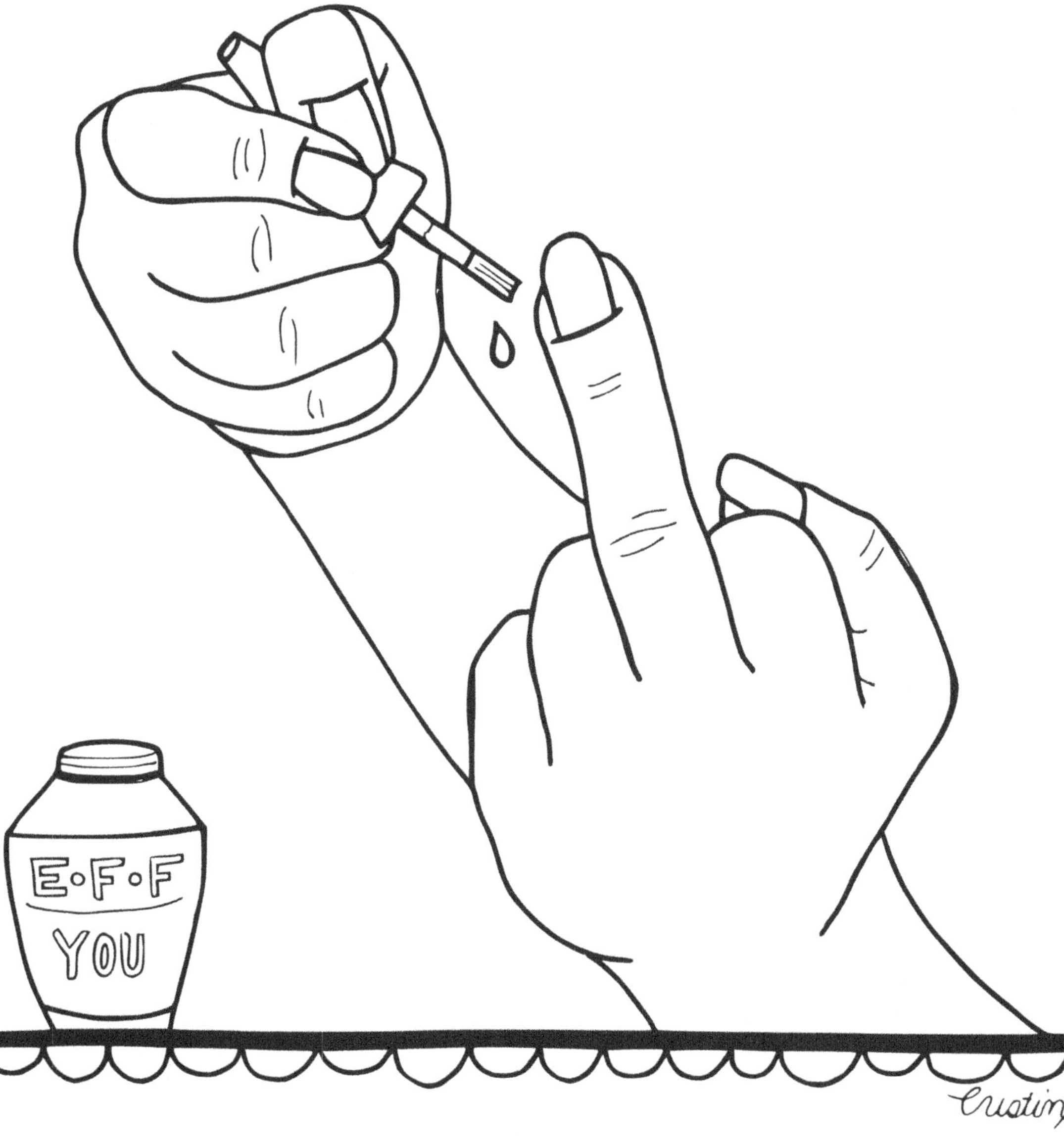

CristinApril.com

The Art of Not Giving A Fuck by Cristin April Frey

Colorist: _____Date: _____

Medium Used: _____

The Art of Not Giving A Fuck by Cristin April Frey

Colorist: _____ Date: _____

Medium Used: _____

The Art of Not Giving A Fuck by Cristin April Frey

Colorist: _____ Date: _____

Medium Used: _____

The Art of Not Giving A Fuck by Cristin April Frey

Colorist: _____Date: _____

Medium Used: _____

Looks like it's
fuck
this
shit
o'clock !

CristinApril.com

The Art of Not Giving A Fuck by Cristin April Frey

Colorist: _____ Date: _____

Medium Used: _____

CristinApril.com

The Art of Not Giving A Fuck by Cristin April Frey

Colorist: _____Date: _____

Medium Used: _____

Well, la dee fucking da.

CristinApril.com

The Art of Not Giving A Fuck by Cristin April Frey

Colorist: _____ Date: _____

Medium Used: _____

Let me write that in my things I don't give a shit about notebook.

CristinApril.com

The Art of Not Giving A Fuck by Cristin April Frey

Colorist: _____Date: _____

Medium Used: _____

The Art of Not Giving A Fuck by Cristin April Frey

Colorist: _____Date: _____

Medium Used: _____

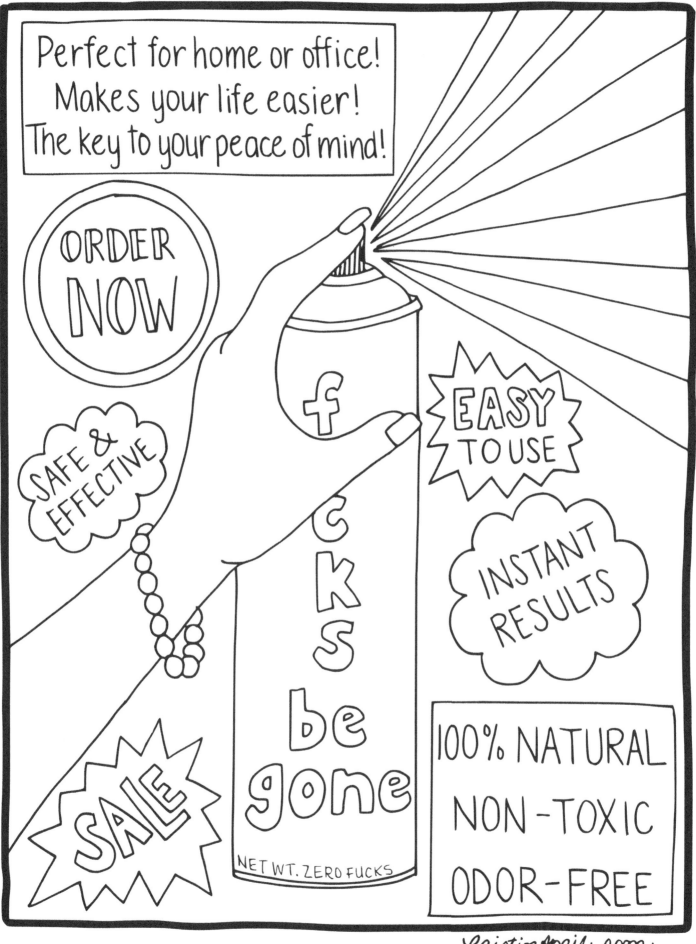

The Art of Not Giving A Fuck by Cristin April Frey

Colorist: _____Date: _____

Medium Used: _____

CristinApril.com

The Art of Not Giving A Fuck by Cristin April Frey

Colorist: _____ Date: _____

Medium Used: _____

Bonus Pages

After receiving so many requests for custom sayings, and not being able to keep up with all of them, I have decided to give you the tools to create your own! The following pages have my personal hand-drawn font for you. Simply trace the letters onto a blank page and then doodle it to create your own custom sweary pages!

abcdefghi

jklmnopqr

stuvwxyz

1234567890

! ; : & * ( )

ABCDEFG

HIJKLMN

OPQRST

UVWXYZ

Colorist: _____Date: _____

Medium Used: _____

Colorist: _____Date: _____

Medium Used: _____

ZEN
AS
FUCK

©CristinApril.com

Colorist: _____Date: _____

Medium Used: _____

Colorist: _____Date: _____

Medium Used: _____

Colorist: _____ Date: _____

Medium Used: _____

Colorist: _____Date: _____

Medium Used: _____

© CristinApril.com

Colorist: _____Date: _____

Medium Used: _____

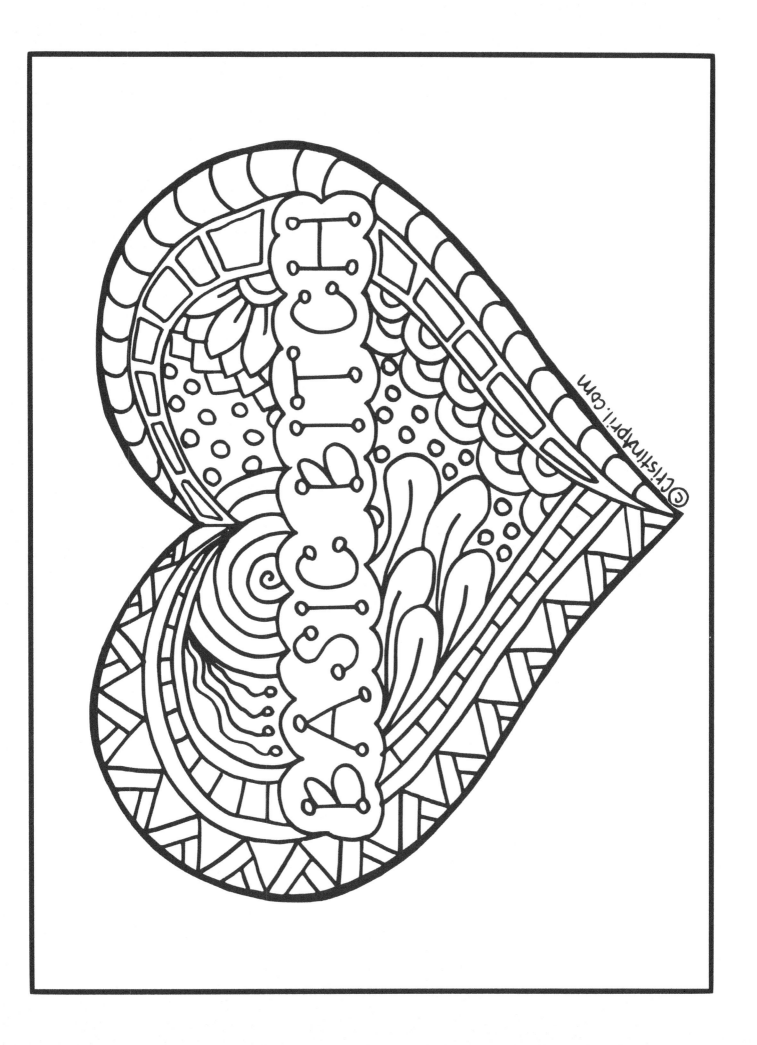

Colorist: _____Date: _____

Medium Used: _____

Colorist: _____Date: _____

Medium Used: _____

Blotter Page

Tear these pages out and place them behind the page you're coloring to
prevent markers from bleeding through to the next picture.
You can also use them to test your colors on first!

Blotter Page

Tear these pages out and place them behind the page you're coloring to
prevent markers from bleeding through to the next picture.
You can also use them to test your colors on first!

Blotter Page

Tear these pages out and place them behind the page you're coloring to
prevent markers from bleeding through to the next picture.
You can also use them to test your colors on first!

Color Palette Practice Sheet

Test your colors here to see if they go well together in a color scheme.

Made in the USA
Coppell, TX
10 December 2019